QUIZPEDIA

HANNAH KOELMEYER

THE
90s

THE ULTIMATE BOOK OF TRIVIA

Smith Street Books

SO YOU THINK YOU KNOW ...

WORLD EVENTS

Quiz 01

1.
What kind of "bug" was the Y2K problem also known as?

2.
In what year was the European Union formally established when the Maastricht Treaty came into force?

3.
Nelson Mandela was released from prison in 1990 and went on to become president of what country?

4.
What dance craze took over the charts courtesy of Los Del Mar?

5.
Euro Disney opened in 1992, outside what capital city?

6.
The Gulf War was led by the US against Iraq in response to Iraq's invasion of what country?

7.
Who became the first president of Russia after the Soviet Union dissolved in 1990?

8.
Who made the first solo flight across the Pacific Ocean in a hot air balloon in 1995?

9.
Which two countries signed the Wadi Araba Treaty in 1994?

10.
Who succeeded North Korean leader Kim Il-sung after his death in 1994?

SO YOU THINK
YOU KNOW ...

BOOKS
FOR KIDS

Quiz 02

1.
What is the fantasy trilogy by Philip Pullman that begins with 1995's *Northern Lights*?

2.
What was the first book in R.L. Stine's *Goosebumps* series, published in 1992?

3.
Released in 1990, which Dr. Seuss book was the last to be published during his lifetime?

4.
Lemony Snicket is the pen name of what American novelist?

5.
What is the name of author Julia Donaldson's monster, a fantastic beast invented by a mouse to avoid being eaten?

6.
What was the *Baby-Sitters Club* spin-off series that focussed on Dawn Schafer and friends after her return to California?

7.
Complete the title of Stephen Chbosky's 1999 coming-of-age novel, *The Perks of Being a ...*

8.
In *Harry Potter and the Philosopher's/Sorcerer's Stone*, who gives Harry his letter of acceptance into Hogwarts on his eleventh birthday?

9.
Name the protagonist of Garth Nix's *The Old Kingdom/Abhorsen* series.

10.
Who is the author of dystopian novel *The Giver*?

SO YOU THINK YOU KNOW ...

THE

SIMPSONS

"D'OH!"

Quiz 03

1.
Who is credited as the creator of *The Simpsons*?

2.
Which US president once called out *The Simpsons* as an undesirable example of an American family, suggesting families should be "a lot more like the Waltons and a lot less like the Simpsons"?

3.
What famous American punk band sang "Happy Birthday" to Mr. Burns?

4.
What was Bart Simpson's catchphrase?

5.
The opening theme music was written by which famous movie soundtrack composer?

6.
Who shot Mr. Burns?

7.
In 1997, *The Simpsons* surpassed what TV show to become the longest-running prime-time animated series in the US?

8.
Which actor, who voiced iconic characters Troy McClure and Lionel Hutz, was tragically killed by his wife in a murder–suicide?

9.
The Simpsons' annual recurring Halloween special is called what?

10.
Which late-night talk show host was formerly a writer on *The Simpsons*:
a. Jimmy Fallon
b. Conan O'Brien
c. David Letterman?

SO YOU THINK
YOU KNOW ...

WOMEN'S
FASHION

Quiz 04

1.
What name was given to stretchy plastic chokers?

2.
What would you call a fabric-covered hair-tie, often made of satin or velvet?

3.
What other name were three-quarter-length capri pants known by?

4.
What strappy dress, often made from satin or other light fabric cut on the bias, was inspired by a piece of underwear?

5.
Who designed the safety pin dress worn by Elizabeth Hurley to the premiere of *Four Weddings and a Funeral*?

6.
What style of pants, often camo print or khaki, had an excess of pockets?

7.
Inspired by Peter Lindbergh's iconic British *Vogue* cover shoot, who were the original "Big Five" supermodels who appeared in George Michael's "Freedom! '90" music video?

8.
Which decade of fashion had a big revival in the 90s, seeing the return of platform shoes and flares?

9.
What layered hairstyle ruled the 90s thanks to Jennifer Aniston?

10.
Which pushup bra became famous in the 90s?

SO YOU THINK
YOU KNOW ...

VIDEO
GAMES

Quiz 05

1.
What was the name of the Nintendo console that was the main rival to the Sega Genesis/Mega Drive?

2.
What was the name of *Street Fighter II*'s sumo wrestler?

3.
Sonic the Hedgehog's Dr. Ivo Robotnik stole six what?

4.
Matches in *Mortal Kombat* featured a gruesome finishing move called what?

5.
In *Super Mario World*, the collection of what power-up gives Mario or Luigi a yellow cape?

6.
What was Lara Croft's occupation?

7.
During which war was *Wolfenstein 3D* set?

8.
StarCraft was published by which American video game developer?

9.
Available in Japan in December of the previous year, Sony released the PlayStation in North America, Europe and Australia in what year?

10.
What ancient wind instrument featured in the title of the *Legend of Zelda* game released in 1998?

SO YOU THINK
YOU KNOW ...

SPORT

Quiz 06

1.
In what cities were the 1992 and 1996 Summer Olympics held?

2.
Name the tennis player who was stabbed during a match in Hamburg in 1993.

3.
How old was Tiger Woods when he became the youngest-ever winner of the Masters in 1997?

4.
Mike Tyson memorably did what to heavyweight challenger Evander Holyfield during a rematch in 1997?

5.
In what year did the now-disgraced Lance Armstrong win his first Tour de France?

6.
Ice skater Tonya Harding's then-husband organized an attack on which skater at the 1994 US Figure Skating Championship?

7.
Who did 17-year-old Serena Williams beat to win her first Grand Slam title?

8.
Which team dominated the NFL in the 90s, winning three Super Bowls over four years?

9.
In what year did the United States host the FIFA World Cup?

10.
What Formula One motor race resulted in the tragic deaths of Ayrton Senna and Roland Ratzenberger?

SO YOU THINK YOU KNOW ...

INDIE

MOVIES

"THE DUDE ABIDES!"

Quiz 07

1.
For what rumored transgression does *Pulp Fiction*'s Marsellus Wallace throw Antwan "Tony Rocky Horror" Roccamora out the window?

2.
In what city do Ethan Hawke and Julie Delpy fall in love in *Before Sunrise*?

3.
In which movie do we first meet Jay and Silent Bob?

4.
Name the six color-related "Mr." aliases used in *Reservoir Dogs*.

5.
Which actress featured in the movie *Scream*'s promotional posters despite her character being killed off in the film's opening sequence?

6.
Who is *Empire Records* star Liv Tyler's rock star father?

7.
What was the profession of John Cusack's character Craig Schwartz in *Being John Malkovich*?

8.
In *The Big Lebowski* what is The Dude's drink of choice?

9.
Which real-life brothers play a pair of troublemaking garbage men in *Men at Work*?

10.
Name the 1999 film of the real-life story of Brandon Teena, for which lead actress Hilary Swank was awarded the Best Actress Academy Award.

SO YOU THINK
YOU KNOW ...

TOYS

Quiz 08

1.
What device was released by Tiger Electronics in 1997 in an attempt to copycat the Tamagotchi?

2.
Which toy featured red and blue boxing robots?

3.
Toy maker Hasbro was sued by Warner Bros. due to what toy's resemblance to the Mogwai from the *Gremlins* movies?

4.
Who lived in a plastic clamshell case that folded out to a mini dollhouse?

5.
Which toys featured five teenagers who transformed into superheroes with costumes in red, pink, black, yellow and blue?

6.
Hailing from the 1960s, what short, colorful-haired toys had a surge of popularity in the 90s?

7.
Name the stuffed toys filled with plastic pellets that are now highly valued as collectibles.

8.
Fill in the blank: This handheld electronic game instructed you to "Twist it, pull it, ----"

9.
Which water gun was originally marketed as the Power Drencher?

10.
What spinning dolls were recalled after the manufacturer received more than 100 complaints of injury?

SO YOU THINK YOU KNOW ...

THE

SPICE

GIRLS

"SPICE UP YOUR LIFE!"

Quiz 09

1.
What are the Spice Girls' real names?

2.
What was the group's original name?

3.
Which magazine gave the group members their famous nicknames?

4.
According to the lyrics of "Stop," the Spice Girls need somebody with what?

5.
In "Spice Up Your Life" do you shake it to the left or the right?

6.
What was the name of the Spice Girls movie?

7.
What was the name of their debut single?

8.
The music video for which single featured the Spice Girls animated as fairies?

9.
Which band member left the group in 1998?

10.
What was the name of the group's third and final album?

STEVEN SPIELBERG

Quiz 10

1.
1991's *Hook* was a retelling of what classic children's book?

2.
What did the scientists do to prevent the Jurassic Park dinosaurs from reproducing?

3.
Who played Oskar Schindler, the lead role in *Schindler's List*?

4.
What is the name of the studio that Spielberg formed in 1994 with Jeffrey Katzenberg and David Geffen?

5.
Released in 1997, what was the title of the sequel to *Jurassic Park*?

6.
Which former US president did Anthony Hopkins play in the historical epic *Amistad*?

7.
How many Academy Award nominations did *Saving Private Ryan* receive?

8.
Which visual effects house created *Jurassic Park*'s ground-breaking special effects?

9.
Saving Private Ryan's epic 20-plus-minute scene depicts a landing on what beach in Normandy?

10.
What actress did Steven Spielberg marry in 1991?

SO YOU THINK YOU KNOW ...

BOOKS FOR ADULTS

Quiz 11

1.
What confounding 1996 post-modern classic is more than 1000 pages long, with one-tenth of that bulk taking the form of endnotes?

2.
How many of George R.R. Martin's novels from the main *A Song of Ice and Fire* series were first published in the 90s?

3.
Who wrote the novel *Jurassic Park*?

4.
Trainspotting, released in 1993, was Irvine Welsh's a. first b. second c. last novel?

5.
Who wrote the novel that popularized the term "Generation X"?

6.
Rob Fleming, the protagonist of Nick Hornby's *High Fidelity*, runs what business?

7.
Complete the title of Haruki Murakami's novel *The Wind-Up ...*

8.
Frank McCourt's memoir *Angela's Ashes* details his young life primarily in which two locations?

9.
What is the name of Bret Easton Ellis' lead character in *American Psycho*?

10.
What classic work of literature is Helen Fielding's *Bridget Jones's Diary* roughly based on?

Quiz 12

1.
What was the name of Sony's portable CD player?

2.
The original iMac G3 was released in what distinctive color?

3.
Which company released the StarTAC, the world's first flip phone?

4.
What open source operating system was created by Linus Torvalds in 1991?

5.
The first text message was sent by a Vodafone engineer in 1992. What did it say?

6.
What does "CD-ROM" stand for?

7.
What does SMS stand for?

8.
The world's first commercial MP3 player, the MPMan, was developed in what country?

9.
The Iomega Zip drive was a revelation in storage compared to standard floppy disks. How much data could the original Zip disk hold?

10.
What type of "Pilot" was a "personal digital assistant" operated using a stylus?

SO YOU THINK
YOU KNOW ...

TITANIC

"I'M THE KING OF
THE WORLD"

Quiz 13

1.
How many Academy Awards did *Titanic* win?

2.
Who played Rose's fiancé Cal Hockley?

3.
Leonardo DiCaprio's Jack wins his ticket to board the *Titanic* playing what game?

4.
By what fake working title was the film referred to during production in order to keep its subject matter secret?

5.
At the time of its release, *Titanic* was the most expensive movie ever made. What was the budget: a. $90 million b. $150 million c. $200 million?

6.
In real life, who actually drew the nude sketch of Rose that was used in the film?

7.
What is the name of the rare diamond set in Rose's necklace?

8.
Who sang the movie's iconic chart-busting theme song "My Heart Will Go On"?

9.
True or false? The movie's famous line, "I'm the king of the world!" was improvised by Leonardo DiCaprio.

10.
Who played the character of the "Unsinkable Molly Brown"?

SO YOU THINK
YOU KNOW ...

SEINFELD

Quiz 14

1.
What is the name of the cafe the *Seinfeld* characters frequent?

2.
Which of the main characters does not appear in the first episode?

3.
What is Kramer's first name?

4.
A Festivus celebration includes the airing of what?

5.
What is the name of George's fake company?

6.
What was creator Larry David's motto for the show, ensuring there would be no sentimentality or character growth?

7.
What is Newman's job?

8.
How does George's fiancée, Susan, die?

9.
How many episodes of *Seinfeld* are there?

10.
What are Jerry's parents' names?

SO YOU THINK
YOU KNOW ...

Quiz 15

1.

What astronomical tool was launched into low Earth orbit by the Space Shuttle *Discovery* in 1990?

2.

A complex repair mission was launched in 1993 to fix what part of the Hubble Telescope?

3.

Where did NASA land *Pathfinder*, the first operational rover on another planet?

4.

The International Space Station (ISS) was launched in what year?

5.

The first photograph of the whole Solar System was taken in 1990 by what spacecraft?

6.

In 1995 the space probe *Galileo* completed the first orbit of what planet?

7.

In 1990 a huge crater in Mexico was identified as the result of an asteroid strike. What major event in Earth's history is this widely believed to have caused?

8.

John Glenn became the oldest human to travel in space in 1998. How old was he: a. 67 b. 77 c. 82?

9.

What gaming device did Aleksandr A. Serebrov play on the Soyuz TM-17 mission to *Mir* in 1993?

10.

Discovered in 1995, *51 Pegasi b* was the first what?

BOY
BANDS

Quiz 16

1.
Of what group was Justin Timberlake formerly a member?

2.
What was the name of Boyz II Men's first album?

3.
Who is the youngest Hanson brother?

4.
Actor Mark Wahlberg's older brother Donnie was a founding member of what band?

5.
Which member of Boyzone went on to a successful solo career, singing the hit "When You Say Nothing At All"?

6.
What country do Westlife come from?

7.
What was the name of the band created by the team who managed the Spice Girls, as an attempt to create a male version of the phenomenon?

8.
In what year did Robbie Williams leave Take That?

9.
East 17 had a hit with a cover of what song by the Pet Shop Boys?

10.
Which group won a Grammy in 1995 for Best Pop Performance by a Duo or Group with Vocal with the song "I Swear"?

SO YOU THINK
YOU KNOW ...

FRIENDS

"PIVOT! PIVOT!"

Quiz 17

1.
Name the actors who portray the six main characters: Monica, Ross, Phoebe, Chandler, Rachel and Joey.

2.
What is Ross' reason for believing he didn't cheat on Rachel?

3.
What is Monica Geller's occupation?

4.
What is the name of the coffee shop frequented by the characters?

5.
Joey Tribbiani gets his big break playing what character on *Days of Our Lives*?

6.
In the pilot episode, Rachel Greene first appears wearing what?

7.
What is Phoebe's twin sister's name?

8.
Chandler once entered (and won) a lookalike competition for what 90s rapper?

9.
The catchy theme song, "I'll Be There For You," is by what duo?

10.
On which network did *Friends* originally air?

THE BRITISH ROYAL FAMILY

Quiz 18

1.
What term did Queen Elizabeth II use to describe the year 1992?

2.
True or false? Prince Charles admitted to adultery in a 1994 television interview.

3.
What was the name of Princess Anne's first husband?

4.
Which of Sarah, Duchess of York (aka Fergie) and Prince Andrew's daughters was born in 1990?

5.
"Squidgygate" was a tabloid scandal that published recorded phone conversations between which two people?

6.
In 1992 a fire caused extensive damage to which of the Queen's residences?

7.
Which royal reporter wrote the biography *Diana: Her True Story*?

8.
Paparazzi photos of the recently separated Sarah, Duchess of York, were published in the tabloid press causing a great scandal, allegedly showing American financial manager John Bryan doing what?

9.
On what date was Princess Diana tragically killed?

10.
In what city did she die?

SO YOU THINK YOU KNOW ...

THE WORLD WIDE WEB

Quiz 19

1.
In what year did Google officially launch?

2.
And what name did creators Larry Page and Sergey Brin originally give the search engine?

3.
Who invented the World Wide Web?

4.
What "Navigator" was an early web browser?

5.
What American web services company began as one of the internet's earliest directories, originally called "Jerry and David's guide to the World Wide Web"?

6.
What does HTTP stand for?

7.
What was the internet originally called until it was renamed in 1990?

8.
What was AOL's chat program called?

9.
If someone requested your A/S/L, what were they asking for?

10.
What aquatic activity used to be a synonym for browsing the internet?

GRUNGE AND ALT ROCK

Quiz 20

1.
In what city was grunge born?

2.
What was the name of Nirvana's second album, which contained their first mainstream hit "Smells Like Teen Spirit"?

3.
Who was the lead singer of Soundgarden?

4.
What is the name of the four-day music festival in Chicago's Grant Park, launched in 1991 by Jane's Addiction singer Perry Farrell?

5.
Courtney Love was lead singer of what band that released four albums?

6.
What is the name of the band Mike Patton formed in high school prior to joining Faith No More?

7.
Which two iconic grunge bands made a cameo in the Cameron Crowe film *Singles*?

8.
What was the name of the Smashing Pumpkins' double album released in 1995?

9.
What was the Rage Against the Machine song "Killing in the Name" written about?

10.
On what album was Radiohead's hit "Creep" released?

SO YOU THINK YOU KNOW ...

CELEBRITY COUPLES

"YOU COMPLETE ME"

Quiz 21

1.
On what movie did Brad Pitt and Gwyneth Paltrow meet?

2.
Matt Damon broke up with Minnie Driver by declaring he was single on what television show?

3.
What mega star did Matthew Perry briefly date after she guest starred on *Friends*?

4.
Which actor Wilson brother did Drew Barrymore date for two years?

5.
For how many days were Carmen Electra and Dennis Rodman married: a. two b. nine c. 18?

6.
Who did a married Ted Danson date in 1992, resulting in a $30 million divorce?

7.
True or false? Madonna dated Vanilla Ice in the early 90s.

8.
Brooke Shields married which tennis star in 1997?

9.
Name the indie film directors who dated (and later married) after meeting on the set of Sonic Youth's music video for "100%"?

10.
Which actress did Ellen DeGeneres meet at a Vanity Fair Oscars party and then date for three-and-a-half years?

SO YOU THINK YOU KNOW ...

FOOD AND DRINK

Quiz 22

1.
What type of Italian bread redefined sandwiches in the 90s?

2.
Which clear soft drink made by PepsiCo was sabotaged by Coca-Cola's release of Tab Clear?

3.
What cocktail was popularized by the TV show *Sex and the City*?

4.
What extremely sour candy was invented in Taiwan in 1975 but was first imported to the US in 1993?

5.
What humble Italian preserved vegetable became (arguably) the biggest food trend of the 90s?

6.
What was New Coke rebranded as in 1992?

7.
What coffee chain created their own drink sizes: tall, grande and venti?

8.
Popularized largely by Jay-Z, which brand of Champagne became the drink of choice for hip-hop artists and was the main ingredient in Tupac Shakur's Thug Passion cocktail?

9.
Which company first introduced the stuffed crust pizza?

10.
What was the most popular salad dressing in the US in 1992?

SO YOU THINK
YOU KNOW ...

KEANU
CLASSICS

Quiz 23

1.
Who directed Keanu
as Johnny Utah in
Point Break?

2.
Name the two Keanu films
from the 90s that feature
a US state in the title.

3.
In what year was *The
Matrix* released?

4.
In the movie *Speed*, the
bus cannot go below what
speed, in order to prevent
a bomb going off?

5.
Who played Dracula
to Keanu's fresh-faced
Jonathan Harker in *Bram
Stoker's Dracula*?

6.
What was the title of
the sequel to *Bill & Ted's
Excellent Adventure*?

7.
In 1993, Keanu starred
in an adaptation of which
Shakespeare play?

8.
In what film did Keanu
play opposite Al Pacino?

9.
Johnny Mnemonic was
adapted from a book
of the same name
by which pioneering
cyberpunk author?

10.
Who replaced Keanu
as the lead in *Speed 2:
Cruise Control* after Keanu
turned the movie down?

SO YOU THINK
YOU KNOW ...

THE

SHOES

Quiz 24

1.
What name was given to the clear plastic (often glittery) women's shoes that were big in the 90s?

2.
Which number Air Jordan were released the year Michael Jordan retired?

3.
With what activity would you associate shoe brands Airwalk, Dekline, Etnies and Hawk Shoes?

4.
What girl's name is used to describe a round-toed shoe with a buckled strap?

5.
The 1992 film *Juice* includes a montage of Omar Epps' character trying on different pairs of what kind of shoe before meeting up with Tupac?

6.
Which brand created the Slinky Platform Sandal?

7.
What fruit was used to describe the red Dr. Martens boots?

8.
Name the brand of Original Universal Active Sandal that you'd see on the feet of Colorado River guides as well as crunchy hacky sack–playing Deadheads and Phish Phans.

9.
Which brand released the chunky Disruptor shoe?

10.
What type of shoe was Whoopi Goldberg wearing under her habit in the promotional posters for *Sister Act* and *Sister Act 2*?

SO YOU THINK YOU KNOW ...

THE DISNEY RENAISSANCE

"EVERYTHING THE LIGHT TOUCHES ..."

Quiz 25

1.
Who is the villain in
Beauty and the Beast?

2.
Who voiced the Genie
in *Aladdin?*

3.
For which song did
Pocahontas win an
Academy Award for Best
Original Song in 1995?

4.
Mulan was based on the
legend of Hua Mulan,
a folk heroine from
what country?

5.
Which famous musical
artist wrote and
performed the songs
in *Tarzan?*

6.
What is the title of the
sequel to *The Rescuers?*

7.
*The Hunchback of Notre
Dame* is based on a
classic novel by which
French author?

8.
Who does Simba fall in
love with in *The Lion King?*

9.
Which 90s animated
Disney movie is set in
Ancient Greece?

10.
What Disney animation
studio released its first
feature length film, *Toy
Story,* in 1995?

SO YOU THINK
YOU KNOW ...

FORREST

GUMP

Quiz 26

1.
In what year was *Forrest Gump* released in theaters?

2.
According to Forrest's mama, why is life like a box of chocolates?

3.
Where do Forrest and Jenny first meet?

4.
How many Academy Awards did *Forrest Gump* win?

5.
After graduating from college, Forrest enlists in the US Army and is sent to fight in what war?

6.
Who directed the film?

7.
Who is interviewed alongside Forrest on *The Dick Cavett Show*?

8.
Which superstar musician is inspired by young Forrest's jerky dance moves?

9.
Into what company does Lieutenant Dan invest his and Forrest's money, making them both millionaires?

10.
Which actress plays the adult Jenny?

SO YOU THINK YOU KNOW ...

RAP AND HIP-HOP

Quiz 27

1.
Was Notorious B.I.G. East Coast or West Coast?

2.
Which influential record label featured artists such as Dr. Dre, Tupac and Snoop Dogg?

3.
How old was Tupac Shakur when he was killed?

4.
What was the name of the Wu-Tang Clan's debut album, widely considered one of the greatest hip-hop albums of all time?

5.
Chuck D and Flavor Flav were the founding members of what group?

6.
Which of A Tribe Called Quest's singles from their third album *Midnight Marauders* was used as the opening theme song for the sitcom *The Wayans Bros.*?

7.
According to the lyrics of the Beastie Boys' "Intergalactic," they like their sugar with what?

8.
What was the title of Nas' acclaimed debut album?

9.
What was the name of the DJ who was the third member of Salt-N-Pepa?

10.
What is Puff Daddy's real name?

SO YOU THINK YOU KNOW ...

THE GOLDEN AGE OF ROM COMS

Quiz 28

1.
Who played the roles of Vivian Ward, Julianne Potter, Anna Scott and Maggie Carpenter?

2.
Tom Cruise's Jerry Maguire had Renée Zellweger's Dorothy at what?

3.
Who won an Academy Award for his role as a gruff novelist with OCD living in New York City who falls for a waitress played by Helen Hunt?

4.
Which two Nora Ephron–penned classics paired Tom Hanks and Meg Ryan as romantic leads?

5.
Who wrote and directed *Chasing Amy*?

6.
In *There's Something About Mary*, what does Mary think she's putting in her hair?

7.
In what city does *While You Were Sleeping* take place?

8.
Name the two iconic rom coms written by screenwriter Richard Curtis released in the 90s.

9.
Who played the title role in the 1996 adaptation of Jane Austen's *Emma*?

10.
Drew Barrymore and Adam Sandler have played opposite each other in three films. What was the first, released in 1998?

SO YOU THINK
YOU KNOW ...

SCIENCE

Quiz 29

1.
What type of dinosaur is Sue, the largest and best preserved skeleton of its kind, discovered in South Dakota in 1990?

2.
Protease inhibitors are a type of antiretroviral drug discovered in the 90s, effective in the treatment of what virus?

3.
Which company released Viagra in 1998?

4.
Russian Cosmonaut Valeri Polyakov returned to Earth in 1995 after spending 437 days in space. Where had he spent his time?

5.
Dolly the clone was what type of animal?

6.
Which international scientific research project was set up to determine the base pairs that make up human DNA?

7.
In 1992 the Climate Change Convention was signed by 154 nations at the Earth Summit held where?

8.
What was the first genetically modified food to be approved for human consumption?

9.
What US car manufacturer produced the EV1 electric car?

10.
In what year did Steve Jobs return to run Apple Computers?

SO YOU THINK YOU KNOW ...

BRITPOP

"WOO HOO!"

Quiz 30

1.
Welsh band Catatonia had a hit with a song that referenced the fictional FBI agents from what TV show?

2.
Which bands were thought of as Britpop's "big four"?

3.
Oasis are from what city?

4.
Which band gave us the singles "Connection," "Waking Up" and "Line Up"?

5.
What was the lead single from Blur's third album, *Parklife*?

6.
Who or what is "the Fuzz" in relation to the Supergrass song, "Caught by the Fuzz"?

7.
In what year did Pulp suggest we all meet up?

8.
The title of the second album released by Suede (or The London Suede as they are known in the US) was: a. *Dog Man Star* b. *Star Dog Man* c. *Man Star Dog*?

9.
What are the first names of Oasis' Gallagher brothers?

10.
Richard Ashcroft was the frontman of what band?

SO YOU THINK
YOU KNOW ...

TEEN
MOVIES

Quiz 31

1.
10 Things I Hate About You is an adaptation of which of Shakespeare's plays?

2.
In which movie did Drew Barrymore play a reporter who poses as a student at her former high school and falls for her teacher?

3.
What color is Cher's iconic tartan plaid Dolce & Gabbana outfit in *Clueless*?

4.
High school jock Zack makes a bet he can turn Laney into what in *She's All That*?

5.
In what movie did Matthew McConaughey utter his famous line, "Alright, alright, alright"?

6.
Which actor's breakout role was playing caveman Link in *Encino Man* (also released as *California Man*)?

7.
Who plays Jim Levenstein's dad in *American Pie*?

8.
Both based on the same French novel, what was the name of the earlier, more faithful film adaptation starring John Malkovich, which preceded the movie *Cruel Intentions*?

9.
Jennifer Love Hewitt was a huge teen star of the 90s largely thanks to her role in what TV drama?

10.
Who directed *Scream*?

SO YOU THINK
YOU KNOW ...

BUSINESS

Quiz 32

1.
What was eBay called when it launched in 1995?

2.
The Mall of America, the largest shopping mall in the US, opened in what city in 1992?

3.
Which popular restaurant opened in Moscow in 1990, symbolizing Russia's transition towards a capitalist free market economy?

4.
Excessive stock speculation of internet-related companies in the late 90s caused what "bubble"?

5.
The mid-90s saw the start of an economic boom in Ireland known as what?

6.
The North American Free Trade Agreement (NAFTA), was signed by which US president?

7.
What company launched in 1997 as a service for renting or buying DVDs via mail?

8.
The World Trade Organization (WTO) was formed after what agreement was signed by 123 nations in 1994?

9.
Amazon was founded in 1994 as an online marketplace for what?

10.
True or false? In 1996, Richard Branson launched a wedding dress business called Virgin Brides.

SO YOU THINK
YOU KNOW ...

THE
SUPERNATURAL
ON SCREEN

Quiz 33

1.
What were Mulder and Scully's first names in *The X-Files*?

2.
What fictional high school did Buffy and the Scooby Gang attend in *Buffy the Vampire Slayer*?

3.
Which actress joined the cast of *Charmed* as long-lost half-sister Paige after Shannen Doherty departed the show?

4.
Which film stars Robin Tunney, Fairuza Balk, Neve Campbell and Rachel True as a teenage coven?

5.
Interview with the Vampire was based on a successful novel by which author?

6.
Which of the three film students is the first to disappear in *The Blair Witch Project*?

7.
Who played Morticia Addams in the 1991 film *The Addams Family*?

8.
What form of animation was used in Tim Burton's *The Nightmare Before Christmas*?

9.
Which legendary horror film director produced the TV series *American Gothic*?

10.
What was the name of the successful spin-off series from *Buffy the Vampire Slayer*?

TV HIGH SCHOOL

"GYM WAS CANCELED DUE TO THE EXTREME DEAD GUY IN THE LOCKER"

Quiz 34

1.
What was the nickname of Zack Morris' nerdy friend in *Saved By the Bell*?

2.
If you were obsessing over Jared Leto as Jordan Catalano, what were you watching?

3.
Name the twins whose move from Minneapolis to Beverly Hills forms the premise of *Beverly Hills, 90210*.

4.
What private school did Will Smith attend in *The Fresh Prince of Bel-Air*?

5.
What was unusual about students Max, Michael and Isabel of *Roswell*?

6.
What was the name of the school principal in *Buffy the Vampire Slayer*?

7.
In *Freaks and Geeks*, Lindsay Weir abandons which geeky school club, in favor of hanging out with the "freaks"?

8.
What was the name of Daria's best friend in the animated series *Daria*?

9.
What show was loosely based on a long-running book series of the same name, featuring beautiful blonde identical twins living in California?

10.
In what fictional town do the characters in *Dawson's Creek* reside?

SO YOU THINK
YOU KNOW ...

MOVIE
SOUNDTRACKS

Quiz 35

1.
The producers of *Cruel Intentions* spent almost 10 percent of the film's budget to use what song?

2.
The soundtrack to 1999's *Magnolia* was largely composed of works by what singer–songwriter?

3.
Which of the two Radiohead songs in *Romeo + Juliet* did not appear on the soundtrack album?

4.
True or false? Seal's "Kiss From A Rose" was used in *The NeverEnding Story III* as well as in *Batman Forever*.

5.
"Stay (I Missed You)" by Lisa Loeb was released as the lead single from what movie soundtrack album?

6.
Wayne's World made what song return to the charts 16 years after its release?

7.
Trainspotting opens with what Iggy Pop song?

8.
Steven Tyler sang "I Don't Want to Miss a Thing" for *Armageddon*. What other connection did he have to the film?

9.
What song from what film holds the record for being the best-selling single by a woman in music history?

10.
Who won the Academy Award for Best Original Song and four Grammy Awards for "Streets of Philadelphia" (from the movie *Philadelphia*)?

SO YOU THINK YOU KNOW ...

ACADEMY AWARDS

Quiz 36

1.
Who hosted the ceremony for the first time in 1990?

2.
Which movie won seven Academy Awards in 1991?

3.
For what movie did Steven Spielberg win his first directing Oscar?

4.
For which 1995 movie did Nicolas Cage win the Best Actor Oscar?

5.
Nominated for her work on *The Adventures of Priscilla, Queen of the Desert*, Australian costume designer Lizzy Gardiner arrived at the 1995 Academy Awards wearing a dress made of what?

6.
Name one of the four movies *Shakespeare in Love* beat to win Best Picture in 1998?

7.
For what song was *South Park* creator Trey Parker nominated for an Oscar in 1999?

8.
How many times in the decade was Meryl Streep nominated for Best Actress?

9.
Which movie based on a novel by Michael Ondaatje won the Oscar for Best Picture in 1996?

10.
Pulp Fiction was nominated for seven Academy Awards. How many did it win?

SO YOU THINK YOU KNOW ...

MICHAEL JORDAN

"YOU FEEL BETTER ABOUT THE EFFORT WHEN YOU WIN"

Quiz 37

1.
In what year did Jordan win his first NBA Finals MVP award?

2.
And how many times did he take the award in the decade?

3.
Featuring Jordan, Scottie Pippen, Magic Johnson, Larry Bird and Charles Barkley, what was the 1992 US men's Olympic basketball team known as?

4.
What is Jordan's record for points in a single game?

5.
Following his first retirement in 1994, Jordan played for the Birmingham Barons and what other baseball team?

6.
Jordan's number 23 was retired by the Bulls in 1994 in a ceremony that saw the erection of a sculpture known as what outside the new United Center?

7.
What did Michael Jordan wear to every game underneath his NBA uniform for good luck?

8.
What sports drink launched the "Be Like Mike" ad campaign in 1992?

9.
In what year did Jordan retire from the NBA a second time?

10.
In what film did Jordan star with Bugs Bunny?

SO YOU THINK YOU KNOW ...

POP

DIVAS

Quiz 38

1.
Released in 1993, what is Mariah Carey's best-selling album?

2.
Celine Dion duetted with Peabo Bryson on the title song to what Disney animated film?

3.
How many of the 16 tracks on Shania Twain's phenomenally successful third album *Come On Over* were released as singles?

4.
Gloria Estefan performed in the Super Bowl XXVI halftime show in what year?

5.
From what album was Janet Jackson's hit "That's the Way Love Goes"?

6.
Which hugely successful album by Alanis Morissette was released in 1995?

7.
What was Britney Spears' debut album?

8.
What was Madonna's 1990 world tour called?

9.
The press were constantly pitting Mariah Carey and Whitney Houston against each other, so rumors of their supposed rivalry were quashed when the two recorded what duet?

10.
Complete the title of Annie Lennox's 1992 hit "Walking on ..."

SO YOU THINK
YOU KNOW ...

ARNIE
MOVIES

"I'LL BE BACK"

Quiz 39

1.
In which Batman movie did Arnie star as Mr. Freeze?

2.
What is the name of Arnie's fictional action star in *Last Action Hero*?

3.
In *Terminator 2: Judgment Day*, Arnold's cyborg assassin is sent back to destroy what new model of Terminator?

4.
For what police department is Arnie working undercover in *Kindergarten Cop*?

5.
Who won a Golden Globe Award for Best Actress in a Comedy for her role in *True Lies*?

6.
In which high-concept comedy did Arnie reunite with his *Twins* co-star Danny DeVito?

7.
What toy is workaholic dad Arnie fighting with rival father Myron (played by Sinbad) to acquire on Christmas Eve in *Jingle All the Way*?

8.
On what planet is *Total Recall* set?

9.
In which film does Arnie star as a police detective alongside Gabriel Byrne as Satan?

10.
How many Ivan Reitman-directed films did Arnie appear in during the 90s?

SO YOU THINK YOU KNOW ...

CELEBRITY SCANDALS

Quiz 40

1.
What was the name of the sex worker Hugh Grant was caught with in 1995?

2.
Who was Jennifer Lopez with at an NYC nightclub when shots were fired in 1999?

3.
Who did Michael Jackson secretly marry in 1994?

4.
In a scandalous tapped phone call, what personal item of Camilla Parker Bowles' did Prince Charles say he wanted to be?

5.
Which actor was arrested in 1996 driving his Porsche on Sunset Boulevard naked and in possession of cocaine, heroin and a .357 Magnum?

6.
In what type of car did O.J. Simpson flee police?

7.
Which 26-year-old model made headlines after marrying 89-year-old oil baron J. Howard Marshall II?

8.
In 1991, Julia Roberts fled to Ireland with ex-boyfriend Jason Patric, just days before she was meant to marry who?

9.
Sinead O'Connor scandalously tore up a photo of who on *Saturday Night Live* in 1992?

10.
A leaked sex tape filmed during their honeymoon, shows Pamela Anderson and who?

SO YOU THINK
YOU KNOW ...

THRILLERS

"THE GREATEST TRICK
THE DEVIL EVER PULLED WAS
CONVINCING THE WORLD HE
DIDN'T EXIST"

Quiz 41

1.
Which 1998 neo-noir film featured Matt Dillon, Neve Campbell, Kevin Bacon, Denise Richards, Bill Murray and Theresa Russell?

2.
In what movie does Haley Joel Osment's character, Cole, see dead people?

3.
Starring Michael Douglas in a twist-filled plot, who directed 1997's *The Game*?

4.
Who wrote the novel of which *Misery*, starring Kathy Bates and James Caan, is an adaptation?

5.
What song does Michael Madsen's character in *Reservoir Dogs* play while severing an ear?

6.
Which actress notably crossed and uncrossed her legs in *Basic Instinct*?

7.
What is the name of Harrison Ford's character in *The Fugitive*?

8.
Which rock star appeared in *Fight Club* as Robert "Bob" Paulson?

9.
Who is the serial killer being investigated by the FBI, which leads to Jodie Foster's Clarice Starling seeking insight from Anthony Hopkins' Hannibal Lecter?

10.
Which of the Baldwin brothers starred in *The Usual Suspects*?

SO YOU THINK
YOU KNOW ...

MEN'S
FASHION

Quiz 42

1.
Shirts made out of what type of fabric epitomized grunge style?

2.
What forward-brushed hairstyle was ubiquitous among boy bands?

3.
What style of light weatherproof jacket made of synthetic fabric was popular in super bright colors and graphic patterns?

4.
What accessory did Tupac Shakur make iconic?

5.
How would you wear your overalls in the 90s?

6.
Shaped like a household item, what type of hat was an essential item for anyone trying to master hip-hop style?

7.
What brand of underwear did Mark Wahlberg model?

8.
What is the name of a bag worn clipped around the waist?

9.
What electronics company manufactured the G-Shock watch?

10.
Air Jordans are made by what sports company?

SO YOU THINK
YOU KNOW ...

SITCOMS

"OH, MR. SHEFFIELD!"

Quiz 43

1.
Where was the Fresh Prince from before he moved to Bel-Air?

2.
In *Home Improvement*, Tim "The Tool Man" Taylor is host of what TV show?

3.
In what year did the final episode of *Cheers* air?

4.
For how many seasons did *Everybody Loves Raymond* run?

5.
Before landing her job as a nanny for British Broadway producer Maxwell Sheffield, where was *The Nanny*'s Fran Fine from?

6.
What occupation do the Crane brothers share on *Frasier*?

7.
From what show was the Chicago-set *Family Matters* a spin-off?

8.
In what city is *Full House* set?

9.
Who did Mila Kunis play in *That '70s Show*?

10.
Name the sitcom about four aliens who come to Earth disguised as a human family in order to conduct research for their leader, The Big Giant Head.

BUDDY COP MOVIES

Quiz 44

1.
How many movies are there in the *Lethal Weapon* franchise?

2.
Who plays Zeus Carver, John McClane's reluctant partner in *Die Hard with a Vengeance*?

3.
Which Hong Kong martial artist starred with Chris Tucker in *Rush Hour*?

4.
True or false? Martin Scorsese's mother, Catherine, stars opposite Sylvester Stallone in *Stop! Or My Mom Will Shoot*.

5.
What device do Agents K and J use to erase the memories of people who have witnessed alien activity in *Men in Black*?

6.
Who played the two leads in *Bad Boys*?

7.
What is the name of National Lampoon's *Lethal Weapon* spoof?

8.
What is unusual about Jerry Lee, partner to Michael Dooley in *K-911*?

9.
Which film starring Kevin Kline and Will Smith cost $170 million to make and was nominated for eight Razzie Awards?

10.
Who was sued for trying to back out of a film in which her tough police detective is partnered up with an anthropomorphic Tyrannosaurus named Theodore Rex?

SO YOU THINK YOU KNOW ...

THE

CARTOON

ERA

Quiz 45

1.
Life is like a what,
here in Duckburg,
according to the *Duck
Tales* theme song?

2.
What type of animal
is Splinter, the
*Teenage Mutant Ninja
Turtles*' sensei and
adoptive father?

3.
Name the three
Powerpuff Girls.

4.
Where did the
Animaniacs live?

5.
What are the twins'
names on *Rugrats*:
a. Phil and Lil
b. Bill and Jill
c. Chuckie and Lil?

6.
What type of animal is
Ren Höek from *The Ren &
Stimpy Show*?

7.
What were the five
elemental powers wielded
by the Planeteers in
*Captain Planet and
The Planeteers*?

8.
Who is Dexter's fellow
boy-genius rival in
Dexter's Laboratory?

9.
In what show do two
mice try to take over the
world every night?

10.
Who created *South Park*
with Trey Parker?

Answers

Quiz 01: 1. The millennium bug 2. 1993 3. South Africa 4. The Macarena 5. Paris 6. Kuwait 7. Boris Yeltsin 8. Steve Fossett 9. Israel and Jordan 10. His son Kim Jong-il

Quiz 02: 1. *His Dark Materials* 2. *Welcome to Dead House* 3. *Oh, the Places You'll Go!* 4. Daniel Handler 5. The Gruffalo 6. *California Diaries* 7. ... *Wallflower* 8. Rubeus Hagrid 9. Sabriel 10. Lois Lowry

Quiz 03: 1. Matt Groening 2. George H.W. Bush 3. Ramones 4. "Eat my shorts" 5. Danny Elfman 6. Maggie Simpson 7. *The Flintstones* 8. Phil Hartman 9. *Treehouse of Horror* 10. b. Conan O'Brien

Quiz 04: 1. Tattoo chokers 2. A scrunchie 3. Pedal pushers 4. Slip dress 5. Gianni Versace 6. Cargo pants 7. Naomi Campbell, Cindy Crawford, Christy Turlington, Linda Evangelista and Tatjana Patitz 8. The 1970s 9. The Rachel 10. Wonderbra

Quiz 05: 1. Super NES (Nintendo Entertainment System; also known as the Super Famicom in Japan and the Super Comboy in South Korea) 2. E. Honda 3. Chaos Emeralds 4. Fatality 5. Cape Feather 6. Archeologist 7. World War II 8. Blizzard Entertainment 9. 1995 10. Ocarina

Quiz 06: 1. Barcelona and Atlanta 2. Monica Seles 3. 21 4. Bit off part of his ear 5. 1999 6. Nancy Kerrigan 7. Martina Hingis 8. Dallas Cowboys 9. 1994 10. 1994 San Marino Grand Prix

Quiz 07: 1. Giving his wife a foot massage 2. Vienna 3. *Clerks* 4. Mr. Brown, Mr. White, Mr. Blonde, Mr. Blue, Mr. Orange and Mr. Pink 5. Drew Barrymore 6. Steven Tyler of Aerosmith 7. Puppeteer 8. A white Russian 9. Emilio Estevez and Charlie Sheen 10. *Boys Don't Cry*

Quiz 08: 1. Giga Pet 2. Rock 'Em Sock 'Em Robots 3. Furby 4. Polly Pocket 5. Mighty Morphin Power Rangers 6. Troll Dolls 7. Beanie Babies 8. Bop It! 9. Super Soaker 10. Sky Dancers

Quiz 09: 1. Melanie Brown, Melanie Chisholm, Emma Bunton, Geri Halliwell and Victoria Beckham (née Adams) 2. Touch 3. *Top of the Pops* 4. A human touch 5. Right 6. *Spice World: The Movie* 7. "Wannabe" 8. "Viva Forever" 9. Geri Halliwell/Ginger Spice 10. *Forever*

Quiz 10: 1. *Peter Pan* 2. They made them all female 3. Liam Neeson 4. DreamWorks 5. *The Lost World: Jurassic Park* 6. John Quincy Adams 7. 11 8. Industrial Light & Magic 9. Omaha Beach 10. Kate Capshaw

Quiz 11: 1. *Infinite Jest* by David Foster Wallace 2. Two: *A Game of Thrones* (1996) and *A Clash of Kings* (1998) 3. Michael Crichton 4. a. first 5. Douglas Coupland 6. A record store 7. ... *Bird Chronicle* 8. Brooklyn, New York and Limerick, Ireland 9. Patrick Bateman 10. *Pride and Prejudice* by Jane Austen

Quiz 12: 1. Discman (later changed to CD Walkman) 2. Bondi blue 3. Motorola 4. Linux 5. Merry Christmas 6. Compact disc read-only memory 7. Short message service 8. South Korea 9. 100 MB 10. Palm

Quiz 13: 1. 11 2. Billy Zane 3. Poker 4. "Planet Ice" 5. c. $200 million 6. Director James Cameron 7. Heart of the Ocean 8. Celine Dion 9. True 10. Kathy Bates

Quiz 14: 1. Monk's 2. Elaine 3. Cosmo 4. Grievances 5. Vandelay Industries 6. No hugging, no learning 7. Mailman 8. From licking cheap envelopes for the wedding invitations 9. 180 10. Morty and Helen

Quiz 15: 1. The Hubble Space Telescope 2. The mirror 3. Mars 4. 1998 5. *Voyager 1* 6. Jupiter 7. Dinosaur extinction 8. b. 77 9. Nintendo Game Boy 10. Exoplanet

Quiz 16: 1. *NSYNC 2. *Cooleyhighharmony* 3. Zac 4. New Kids on the Block 5. Ronan Keating 6. Ireland 7. 5ive 8. 1995 9. "West End Girls" 10. All-4-One

Quiz 17: 1. Courteney Cox, David Schwimmer, Lisa Kudrow, Matthew Perry, Jennifer Aniston and Matt LeBlanc. 2. They were "on a break" 3. Chef 4. Central Perk 5. Dr. Drake Ramoray 6. A wedding dress 7. Ursula 8. Vanilla Ice 9. The Rembrandts 10. NBC

Quiz 18: 1. "Annus horribilis" 2. True 3. Captain Mark Phillips 4. Princess Eugenie 5. Diana, Princess of Wales and James Gilbey (heir to Gilbey's Gin) 6. Windsor Castle 7. Andrew Morton 8. Sucking Fergie's toes 9. August 31, 1997 10. Paris

Quiz 19: 1. 1998 2. BackRub 3. Tim Berners-Lee 4. Netscape 5. Yahoo! 6. Hypertext transfer protocol 7. ARPANET 8. AIM (AOL Instant Messenger) 9. Age, sex, location 10. Surfing

Quiz 20: 1. Seattle 2. *Nevermind* 3. Chris Cornell 4. Lollapalooza 5. Hole 6. Mr. Bungle 7. Alice in Chains and Soundgarden 8. *Mellon Collie and the Infinite Sadness* 9. The Rodney King beating and the LA riots following police acquittal 10. *Pablo Honey*

Quiz 21: 1. *Se7en*
2. *The Oprah Winfrey Show* 3. Julia Roberts
4. Luke 5. b. nine
6. Whoopi Goldberg
7. True 8. Andre Agassi
9. Spike Jonze and Sofia Coppola 10. Anne Heche

Quiz 22: 1. Focaccia
2. Crystal Pepsi
3. The cosmopolitan
4. Warheads 5. Sundried tomato 6. Coke II
7. Starbucks 8. Cristal
9. Pizza Hut 10. Ranch dressing

Quiz 23: 1. Kathryn Bigelow 2. *My Own Private Idaho* and *Feeling Minnesota* 3. 1999
4. 50 miles per hour
5. Gary Oldman 6. *Bill & Ted's Bogus Journey*
7. *Much Ado About Nothing* 8. *The Devil's Advocate* 9. William Gibson 10. Jason Patric

Quiz 24: 1. Jelly sandals 2. Air Jordan IX
3. Skateboarding 4. Mary Jane 5. Reebok Pumps
6. Steve Madden
7. Cherry 8. Teva 9. Fila
10. Red high heels

Quiz 25: 1. Gaston
2. Robin Williams
3. "Colors of the Wind"
4. China 5. Phil Collins
6. *The Rescuers Down Under* 7. Victor Hugo
8. Nala 9. *Hercules*
10. Pixar

Quiz 26: 1. 1994
2. You never know what you're gonna get
3. The school bus 4. Six
5. Vietnam 6. Robert Zemeckis 7. John Lennon
8. Elvis Presley 9. Apple
10. Robin Wright

Quiz 27: 1. East Coast
2. Death Row Records
3. 25 4. *Enter the Wu-Tang (36 Chambers)* 5. Public Enemy 6. "Electric Relaxation" 7. Coffee and cream 8. *Illmatic*
9. Spinderella 10. Sean Combs

Quiz 28: 1. Julia Roberts 2. Hello 3. Jack Nicholson 4. *You've Got Mail* and *Sleepless in Seattle* 5. Kevin Smith
6. Hair gel 7. Chicago
8. *Four Weddings and a Funeral* and *Notting Hill* 9. Gwyneth Paltrow
10. *The Wedding Singer*

Quiz 29: 1. Tyrannosaurus rex 2. HIV 3. Pfizer
4. The *Mir* space station
5. A sheep 6. The Human Genome Project 7. Rio de Janeiro 8. The Flavr Savr tomato 9. General Motors
10. 1996

Quiz 30: 1. *The X-Files* ("Mulder and Scully")
2. Blur, Oasis, Pulp and Suede/The London Suede
3. Manchester 4. Elastica
5. "Girls & Boys" 6. The police 7. 2000 8. a. Dog Man Star 9. Noel and Liam 10. The Verve

Quiz 31: 1. *The Taming of the Shrew* 2. *Never Been Kissed* 3. Yellow
4. Prom queen 5. *Dazed and Confused* 6. Brendan Fraser 7. Eugene Levy
8. *Dangerous Liaisons*
9. *Party of Five* 10. Wes Craven

Quiz 32: 1. AuctionWeb
2. Minnesota 3. McDonald's
4. The dot-com bubble
5. The Celtic Tiger 6. Bill Clinton 7. Netflix 8. The Marrakesh Agreement
9. Books 10. True

Quiz 33: 1. Fox and Dana 2. Sunnydale High
3. Rose McGowan 4. *The Craft* 5. Anne Rice 6. Josh
7. Anjelica Huston 8. Stop motion 9. Sam Raimi
10. *Angel*

Quiz 34: 1. Screech 2. *My So-Called Life* 3. Brenda and Brandon Walsh 4. Bel-Air Academy 5. They were aliens 6. Principal Snyder 7. The mathletes 8. Jane Lane 9. *Sweet Valley High* 10. Capeside

Quiz 35: 1. "Bittersweet Symphony" by The Verve 2. Aimee Mann 3. "Exit Music (For a Film)" 4. True 5. *Reality Bites* 6. "Bohemian Rhapsody" by Queen 7. "Lust for Life" 8. It starred his daughter Liv Tyler 9. "I Will Always Love You" by Whitney Houston from *The Bodyguard* 10. Bruce Springsteen

Quiz 36: 1. Billy Crystal 2. *Dances With Wolves* 3. *Schindler's List* 4. *Dead Poets Society* 5. Gold American Express cards 6. *Elizabeth*, *Life Is Beautiful*, *Saving Private Ryan* and *The Thin Red Line* 7. "Blame Canada" from *South Park: Bigger, Longer & Uncut* 8. Four 9. *The English Patient* 10. One (Best Original Screenplay)

Quiz 37: 1. 1991 2. Six 3. The Dream Team 4. 69 5. The Scottsdale Scorpions 6. "The Spirit" 7. His North Carolina practice shorts 8. Gatorade 9. 1999 10. *Space Jam*

Quiz 38: 1. *Music Box* 2. *Beauty and the Beast* 3. 12 4. 1992 5. *Janet* 6. *Jagged Little Pill* 7. *...Baby One More Time* 8. "Blonde Ambition" 9. "When You Believe" 10. "... Broken Glass"

Quiz 39: 1. *Batman & Robin* 2. Jack Slater 3. The T-1000 4. LAPD 5. Jamie Lee Curtis 6. *Junior* 7. A Turbo-Man action figure 8. Mars 9. *End of Days* 10. Three (*Kindergarten Cop*, *Junior* and a cameo appearance in *Dave*)

Quiz 40: 1. Divine Brown 2. Sean "Puff Daddy" Combes 3. Lisa Marie Presley 4. Her tampon 5. Robert Downey Jr. 6. A white Ford Bronco SUV 7. Anna Nicole Smith 8. Kiefer Sutherland 9. Pope John Paul II 10. Tommy Lee

Quiz 41: 1. *Wild Things* 2. *The Sixth Sense* 3. David Fincher 4. Stephen King 5. "Stuck in the Middle with You" by Stealers Wheel 6. Sharon Stone 7. Dr. Richard Kimble 8. Meat Loaf 9. Buffalo Bill 10. Stephen

Quiz 42: 1. Flannelette 2. The Caesar cut 3. Windbreaker 4. A backwards bandana tied around the head 5. With one strap down 6. Bucket hat 7. Calvin Klein 8. Fanny pack/bum bag 9. Casio 10. Nike

Quiz 43: 1. West Philadelphia 2. *Tool Time* 3. 1993 4. Nine 5. Flushing, Queens 6. Psychiatry 7. *Perfect Strangers* 8. San Francisco 9. Jackie Burkhart 10. *3rd Rock from the Sun*

Quiz 44: 1. Four 2. Samuel L. Jackson 3. Jackie Chan 4. False (the role is played by Estelle Getty) 5. A neuralyzer 6. Will Smith and Martin Lawrence 7. *Loaded Weapon 1* 8. He is a German Shepherd 9. *Wild Wild West* 10. Whoopi Goldberg

Quiz 45: 1. A hurricane 2. A rat 3. Blossom, Bubbles and Buttercup 4. In the water tower on the Warner Bros. studio lot 5. a. Phil and Lil 6. A Chihuahua 7. Fire, earth, wind, water and heart 8. Mandark 9. *Pinky and the Brain* 10. Trey Parker and Matt Stone

"HASTA LA VISTA, BABY"

Smith Street Books

Published in 2021 by Smith Street Books
Naarm | Melbourne | Australia
smithstreetbooks.com

ISBN: 978-1-92241-735-0

Publisher: Paul McNally
Text: Hannah Koelmeyer
Editor: Ariana Klepac
Designer: Vanessa Masci
Layout: Megan Ellis
Project manager: Aisling Coughlan
Cover illustration: Chantel De Sousa

Printed & bound in China by C&C Offset Printing Co., Ltd.

Book 176
10 9 8 7 6 5 4 3 2 1